CANCER

CANCER

by Gail Kay Haines

FRANKLIN WATTS
NEW YORK | LONDON | TORONTO | SYDNEY | 1980
A FIRST BOOK

Photographs courtesy of: American Cancer Society: pp. 11 (by A. Burton), 26, 56 (by Mike Hollander); Martin Rotker/Taurus Photos: pp. 18 (top and bottom), 46 (top and bottom) Memorial Sloan Kettering Cancer Center: p. 39 (top and bottom).

Library of Congress Cataloging in Publication Data

Haines, Gail Kay.
    Cancer.

        (A First book)
        Bibliography: p.
        Includes index.
        SUMMARY: Investigates cancer, the types, warning signs, treatment, and the present state of research in the field.
        1. Cancer—Juvenile literature. [1. Cancer]
I. Title.
RC263.H26   616.99′4   80–14870
    ISBN 0–531–04159–X

Contents

Chapter 1
1 CANCER THE ENEMY

Chapter 2
3 CANCER AND THE CELL

Chapter 3
7 CANCER AND THE BODY

Chapter 4
14 CANCER INVADES

Chapter 5
22 THE CANCER SCOUTS

Chapter 6
28 SURGERY AGAINST CANCER

Chapter 7
31 RADIATION AGAINST CANCER

Chapter 8
36 DRUGS AGAINST CANCER

Chapter 9
43 THE BODY'S OWN DEFENDER CELLS

Chapter 10
50 RESEARCH: FIGHTING FOR THE FUTURE

Chapter 11
54 CANCER AND YOU

58 Glossary
61 For Further Reading
62 Index

CANCER

Chapter 1
CANCER
THE ENEMY

Cancer is the enemy. Cancer is a disease which attacks men, women, and children, plants and animals. It has probably been a dangerous enemy almost since the beginning of life on earth.

No one knows where or when or why the first cancer appeared, but scientists have discovered dinosaur bones and linen-wrapped mummies and even fossils of prehistoric plants which show signs of death due to cancer. Every day, from ancient times to right now, cancer has been claiming victims.

Cancer kills more children than any other disease. Every year in the United States, more than three thousand children die from it. And in adults, only heart disease is deadlier. In 1980, cancer will probably kill 390,000 Americans. Cancer is a powerful enemy indeed.

And in a very strange way, cancer is its own enemy. Once a cancer starts, it grows and grows and grows until it kills its own host animal or plant. Then, because cancer does not seem to be passed from one victim to another, that cancer dies, too.

No one knows why cancer is the enemy of all forms of life, including itself. One of the things that makes cancer so hard to understand is that it is not just one disease. In fact, there are more than one hundred—maybe as many as five hundred—different kinds of cancer. The reason all these illnesses are lumped together under the same name is because they are alike in a very important way. They are all cases of growth gone wild. Cancer has been defined as a "continuous growth in the body which does not follow the normal growth pattern." That means a cancer does not obey the signals which tell different parts of the body what to do and when to stop growing.

How does cancer start? Somehow, something goes wrong with one or more of the body's trillion tiny living units, called cells. Cells taken over by cancer no longer obey the body in which they live. They become "enemy territory." This is where cancer's invasion begins.

Chapter 2
CANCER AND THE CELL

Look at a piece of cork. Use a magnifying glass to see it better. It seems to be made mostly of holes glued together. More than three hundred years ago, a British scientist named Robert Hooke peered into a microscope at a tiny slice of cork and saw a series of neat little pockets that looked like empty rooms. He called the tiny rooms "cells."

The cells in a piece of cork are dead and especially easy to see. Later, other scientists, using better microscopes, discovered live cells in many different materials. They found, in fact, that all living things are made of cells, from flowers to honeybees to humans.

Live, healthy cells are not empty. They are like active factories, using and storing energy, manufacturing products, and reading and copying complicated instructions. They can even divide in half, to make live copies of themselves. Cells come in many different sizes and shapes and do many different jobs. But all cells are alike in a few basic ways.

All cells have an outside covering, called the *cell mem-*

[3

brane (cell wall, in plants). This membrane guards the cell, letting in the food and water and other substances the cell needs and passing waste products and other substances out. The cell membrane also acts as an alarm system for the cell. When it is crowded against other cell membranes, it seems to signal its own cell to stop growing and dividing, unless replacement cells are needed.

Most cell membranes are covered by a coating of sticky molecules. The coating helps glue cells together in a neat, orderly pattern. Inside the membrane is a grayish slimy jelly called *cytoplasm.* All the other parts of the cell float inside the cytoplasm, and it holds or dissolves the chemicals the cell makes and uses.

An electron microscope shows that the cytoplasm contains several different kinds of tiny saclike bodies, called *organelles,* which make or store or use energy and food. Some manufacture important kinds of protein.

But the most important inner part of the cell is the *nucleus.* It is surrounded by its own, double-walled membrane, which protects it the way the cell membrane protects the whole cell. The nucleus is like a tiny computer. It holds enough information to manufacture a whole living body. Whenever the cell divides in two, the nucleus divides first.

Inside, the nucleus is filled with long twisting threads called *chromosomes.* The chromosomes are the "memory banks" of the "computer." They come in pairs, and each kind of animal or plant has a definite number of them in each cell. Normal human cells have twenty-three pairs, or forty-six chromosomes. Chromosomes are actually long chains of subunits called *genes,* which regulate everything about a person from sex to height to shade of eyes. They may also regulate whether or not a person gets cancer.

Genes are built from interlocking pairs of four special chemicals called *nucleotides,* which the body gets from food and vitamins. Nucleotide pairs link together around a central core in long, twisted molecules that look something like spiral staircases. These huge, complicated molecules are called *deoxyribonucleic acid, or DNA.*

Nucleotide pairs can be arranged in different ways into billions of different DNA molecules. Each arrangement has a special meaning. These molecules can store billions of bits of information about the body in a code that all normal cells can read.

When a cell begins to divide, the chromosomes get shorter. They untwist and pull apart sideways, like a ladder cut in half down the middle. Each nucleotide in the chain links up with a new partner-nucleotide, forming two identical new DNA chains. This is the way each half of a dividing cell gets a complete set of chromosomes. The two new "daughter" cells are just alike, except for one thing: Only one of them will ever divide again.

WHEN SOMETHING GOES WRONG

Cancer changes cells in several important ways. They no longer look or act like normal cells. Scientists do not yet completely understand all the things cancer does to a cell. But they are finding out that it seems to make changes in every major part of a cell, from the membrane on the outside to the chromosomes inside the nucleus.

On the outside, the alarm system fails. Crowded cells no longer stop dividing. In fact, cancer cells—that is, cells changed by cancer—keep on dividing until they push everything around them out of place. And cancer cells no longer

[5

seem to have the sticky coating that glues cells to each other. They are free to float away to other parts of the body.

Inside, the cell changed by cancer does not do its normal work. Cancerous white cells can't fight infection, and cancerous kidney cells can't clean the blood. The tiny organelles inside cancer cells make unusual, useless proteins. Also, cancer cells become gluttons for food, taking far more than their share. And then, since the cells cannot use all that extra food, most of it is thrown away.

Inside the nucleus, cancer cells often have extra chromosomes and more DNA than normal cells. Their genes have changed, plugging the wrong information into the cell's "computer," and they pass that wrong information on to two new cells every time they divide. Cancer cells do not actually divide faster than ordinary cells, but they do it much more often. And to make things worse, *both* daughter cells of a cancer cell can divide again. Finally, under a microscope, most cancer cells do not look normal. They may be larger, or have ragged, unusual shapes.

Researchers have many different ideas about how cells become cancers. Chapter 4 will describe some of them. But scientists do know for sure that every cancer starts in a cell. From one or more cells, cancer can launch an invasion to destroy the whole body.

Chapter 3
CANCER AND
THE BODY

Cancer can invade any part of the body. The skin, the lungs, the bones, the sex organs, and almost anywhere can be a starting place.

There is a whole vocabulary of special words doctors use to describe cancer. "Malignant" comes from a Latin word for "evil." To doctors, it means something which will kill the patient if it is not stopped, and it is used as another word for "cancerous." "Benign," the opposite of "malignant," means "not cancerous."

A *tumor* is any unusual growth of extra cells in or on the body. Many tumors (also called growths) are benign, but almost all cancers involve some kind of growth. A doctor who treats cancer is called an oncologist, from a Greek word for "tumor."

Tumors usually have names that end in "oma," but cancerous ones have special names. Malignant growths which grow from any part of the body's lining, including the skin, the inside and outside of the body organs, the glands, the lungs, and the digestive system are all called *carcinomas,* from the Greek word for "crab."

John Roberts, fifty-nine years old, has a carcinoma, but he doesn't know it. He knows that he feels like coughing most of the time, and there is a dull ache, sometimes, on the left side of his chest. John hopes the ache and the coughing will go away soon, but he doesn't feel sick enough, yet, to go to his doctor.

John has a small malignant growth developing on the wall inside his left lung. It has been growing there for several years, and it is doubling in size about every five months. Cells from John's carcinoma have already begun to slip away in the clear, watery lymph, which circulates inside a person's body. Some of the cells have begun to grow another tumor on John's liver.

Melissa Cohen, thirty-nine, also has a carcinoma. She has been losing weight for almost a year, and she feels very tired all the time. Melissa saw her doctor several months ago, but he could find nothing wrong. He told her to get more rest. Now Melissa is so thin her clothes are three sizes too big, and she feels too tired to get out of bed. She is having trouble swallowing, and she can feel a strange lump inside her neck.

Melissa has a carcinoma growing on her thyroid gland, which is a small, butterfly-shaped organ in the neck. The thyroid gland secretes chemicals into the blood which help the body grow and use energy. But Melissa's thyroid is no longer working properly. A few of the cancerous cells have spread to Melissa's lungs.

Janice Hughes, fifty, has a carcinoma, but she doesn't know it. In fact, she feels fine. Janice has made an appointment to see her doctor next week, simply because she has a checkup every year. Janice has a small carcinoma growing on her cervix, which is the entrance to the uterus, where babies develop. It has been growing for almost a year, but it has not spread very far.

About eighty-five out of every hundred human cancers are carcinomas. But carcinomas are only one of the four main kinds of cancer. The second main type is the *sarcomas.* These malignant tumors grow in the muscles, bones, fat, and connective tissues. Only about two cancers in a hundred are sarcomas.

Cancers of the lymph system, the third main type, are called *lymphomas.* Lymph is the clear body fluid which helps blood carry food and waste products. It flows around the body in tubes and collects in tiny pockets called nodes. Cancer cells travel easily through the lymph system, spreading from one place to another. Sometimes the system itself becomes cancerous. About five or six cancers in a hundred are lymphomas.

Three or four cancers in a hundred are *leukemias,* the fourth main kind. Leukemia is the cancer that most often attacks children. It is a cancer of the bone marrow—the spongy red material inside bones, where the body manufactures blood.

Blood is made up of many different particles. Tiny red cells make it look red, as they carry oxygen from the lungs to all parts of the body. A teaspoonful of normal blood has about twenty-five million red cells. Larger white cells fight infection, and the normal blood of a person at rest has about twenty-five thousand of them in a teaspoonful. A third, plate-shaped particle called a platelet helps thicken and clot blood.

White cells are called *leukocytes,* and there are several different kinds of them. When cancer invades bone marrow, the marrow begins producing extra leukocytes—billions of them. Leukemic blood may have as many as three to five million malignant white cells in a teaspoonful of blood. No one knows why. Cancerous white cells never mature. They usually don't look normal under a microscope, and they can't fight infections. They just fill up the blood, crowding out the normal red cells, white cells, and platelets the body needs.

Julie Farrow, nine, has cancer, but she doesn't know it. She knows that she never seems to feel well anymore, and she doesn't have much energy. She thinks this is because she had so many colds this winter. She had two nosebleeds last week, and now she has a strange rash on her legs. Julie has leukemia. Her blood can't fight colds or carry all the oxygen she needs because it is filled with useless cancer cells. Because so many platelets have been crowded out of her blood, Julie is beginning to bleed internally.

Kevin Howard, thirteen, also has cancer. He has been feeling pains in his right leg, just above the knee. This week he noticed that the painful area looks slightly bluish. It feels hot, and it seems to be swelling. Moving it hurts. Kevin knows

Viewed under a microscope, this normal blood sample (left) shows two white cells among many red cells. Blood from a patient with leukemia (right) shows five times as many white cells as are found in the normal blood.

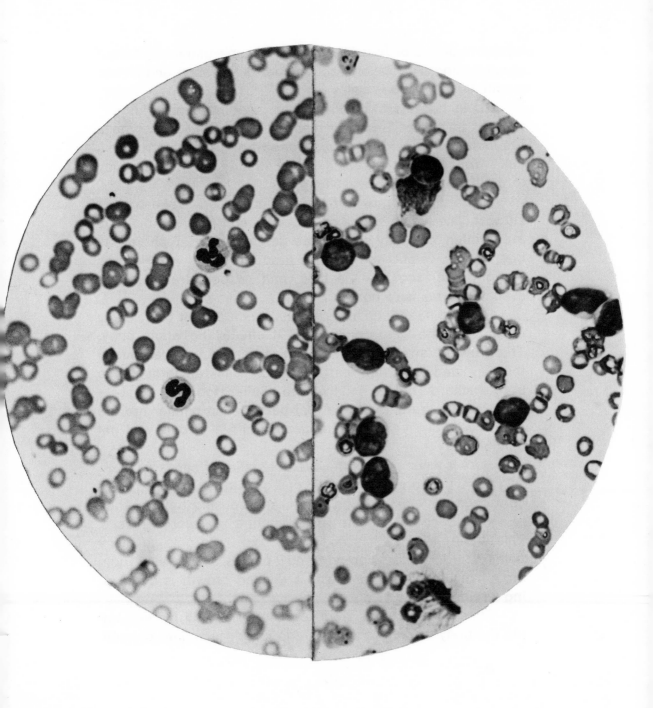

he didn't bruise or hurt his leg, so he can't understand what is happening. He played soccer until the season ended last month and his leg was fine.

Kevin has a fast-growing osteogenic sarcoma ("osteo" means "bone," and "genic" means "growing"). Cancer cells are multiplying inside the long bone of his right thigh. A few cells from Kevin's sarcoma have already made their way through the blood to Kevin's lung.

Richard Waring, twenty-seven, has cancer, but he doesn't know it. The lymph nodes on his neck and between his legs are swollen, and they seem to be getting bigger. Richard has been losing weight, and he feels tired and run down. He runs a slight fever some of the time, and he perspires at night, even when he isn't hot.

Richard has Hodgkin's disease. It is a cancer that seems to begin in the lymph nodes, but it affects the whole body. The growing, swelling nodes push veins and muscles out of the way, and the lymph carries cancer cells all through the body. Richard's spleen and liver are swollen, too.

Richard Waring is not a real person, and neither are the other five. But they are like thousands of real people who get cancer every year.

Here is a summary of the characteristics of cancers.

First, they are uncontrolled cell growth. Clumps of malignant cells are making John cough and causing Kevin's knee to swell. Second, cancers are immature, nonworking cells. This is why Melissa has no energy and Julie gets so many colds. Third, cancers spread to new places. This is why Richard's liver is swollen, and why a second growth is developing on Kevin's lung.

These three effects work together. They kill by weakening the body so much that it can no longer take care of itself.

Sometimes cancer victims die of pneumonia or other infections. Sometimes they die from starvation, because the body can no longer use food. Different cancers affect the body in different ways.

Two out of every three people who get cancer, die from cancer. One out of three can be cured. In fact, doctors have cured hundreds of thousands of cancer patients and made life longer and happier for millions of others. The trouble is, doctors can't help if they don't know a person is sick. If John and Melissa and Janice, Kevin and Julie and Richard do not see a doctor soon, all six will probably die.

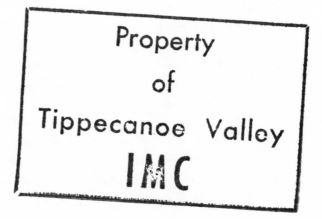

Chapter 4
CANCER INVADES

More than two hundred years ago, a British surgeon named Sir Percival Pott discovered the first "cause" of cancer. He noticed that chimney sweeps often died from cancer of the scrotum, the pouch around the male sex glands. He suspected that their cancers were caused by the soot and coal dust which they didn't bother to wash off. Modern scientists have proved that he was right.

Since then, hundreds of different causes of cancer have been found. Almost every week, the newspaper announces that a new cause has been discovered. It almost seems as if *everything* causes cancer, but that isn't true. Researchers are not sure, but they think there are four main causes of cancer —chemicals, radiation, viruses, and the body itself. Working together or by themselves, these four agents can cause cancer—some of the time. But none of them seem to cause cancer all of the time, in everybody. No one knows why.

CHEMICALS

John Roberts smokes two or three packs of cigarettes every day. He has been smoking since he was a teen-ager and he doesn't want to stop. But now, John has a cancer growing on his lung. Seventy-five years ago, when smoking was rare, lung cancer was rare. Today it is the most common cancer in men and becoming more and more common in women. Almost all of these hundreds of thousands of lung cancer victims have been smoking for ten or fifteen or twenty years.

Cigarette smoke has at least seven *carcinogens* in it. A carcinogen is a chemical or other substance which has been proved to cause cancer. The cells in John's lungs get a carcinogen bath every time he puffs on a cigarette.

Chemical carcinogens usually work slowly. First, they change and weaken cells. These weakened cells are called precancerous cells because they are more likely to turn into cancers than will healthy cells. Five or ten or twenty years later, they may develop into malignant growths.

Many chemicals which can cause cancer are found in factories and other places where people work. Here are a few examples.

People who work in dye-making factories develop cancer of the bladder more often than other people, even if they handle the dyes for only a short time. The cancer usually appears ten years later. Chemists are also prone to bladder cancer, and rubber and plastics workers to cancer of the liver. Researchers suspect that lymphomas and cancer of the pancreas, the kidneys, and other places will one day be traced to chemical carcinogens.

Insulation workers, pipefitters, car mechanics and anyone who works with asbestos, a carcinogen made from ground

[15

rock, may get a special kind of lung cancer called meso-thelioma. Even the families of asbestos workers, who breathe dust from their hair and clothing, sometimes have precancer-ous cells in their lungs.

Researchers have caused cancer in laboratory animals with all these and hundreds of other chemicals. Some scientists think nine out of every ten cancers are caused by chemicals. Most industries are more careful, now, to protect their workers from carcinogenic chemicals. But it may be too late for people who were exposed years ago. They may still get cancer.

And factories are not the only place where people are exposed to carcinogenic chemicals. Teen-age girls whose mothers were given a drug called diethylstilbestrol (DES) before they were born, sometimes develop a cancerous growth in the vagina, or birth canal. This cancer is very rare in other people. And the mothers who took the DES are more likely to get breast cancer.

Worst of all are the carcinogens people give to them-selves. Fatty foods seem to contain or make carcinogens which can cause breast cancer and cancer of the colon. These cancers are the two most common kinds, next to lung cancer, which comes mainly from smoking. Some experts think that smoking cigarettes and eating a high-fat diet may cause more cancer than all the industrial chemicals put together.

VIRUSES

Julie Farrow's leukemia is even more of a mystery. Some scientists think leukemia may be caused by a virus. Viruses are very tiny bits of living, or almost living, matter. (No one knows if viruses are truly alive.) Because they are so small, viruses can get inside and kill healthy cells, causing diseases such as polio, measles, colds, and the flu. Some viruses have a central core of DNA, the material that the chromosomes inside every cell are made of. Others have a core of RNA, a large, message-carrying molecule.

When a virus gets inside a cell, its own core takes over the nucleus. It forces the cell to produce new viruses instead of the things a cell needs to stay alive. When the cell dies, these new viruses go out and attack other cells. Now, scientists are discovering that killing cells may not be the only way a virus can act. Instead, it may replace just a tiny bit of the cell's DNA with a piece of its own called a virogene. For a while, the cell can control the virogene and nothing happens. Then, for reasons scientists do not understand, the virogene begins turning the cell into a cancer. The cancer cell divides into more and more cancer cells, each with a little piece of virogene in its nucleus.

Traces of viruses have often been found in mice with leukemia and even in mice which will get leukemia later. They have also been found in human leukemia patients. Breast cancer victims sometimes have pieces of viruses inside their malignant cells, and so do patients with cancer of the cervix and cancer of the colon. But finding viruses in cancer cells does not prove the virus started the cancer.

Most researchers think it takes more than just a virus to cause a cancer. Perhaps Julie's leukemia and Janice's cancer of the cervix were started by a virus and helped along by something else. That may be how all cancers begin. No one knows for sure.

[17

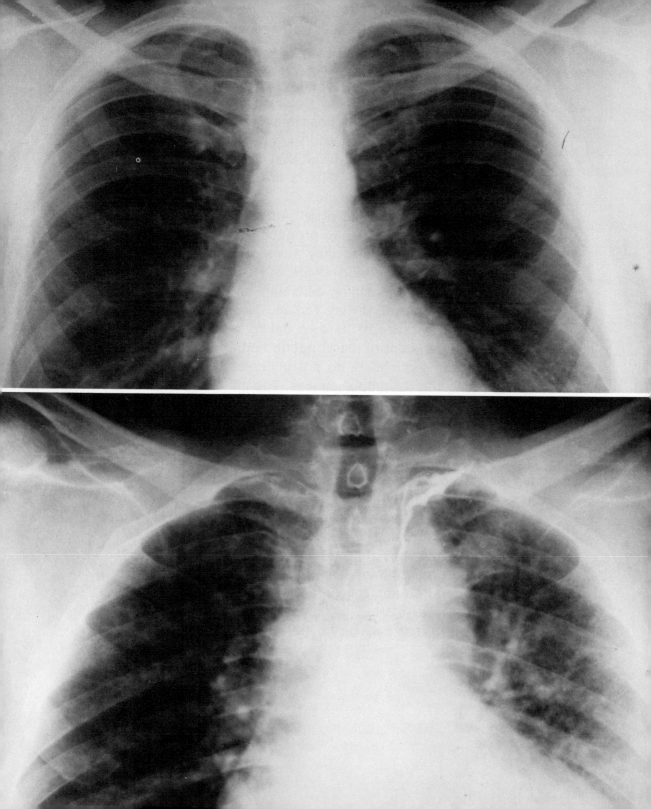

RADIATION

Radiation is another cancer causer. In fact, many of the early researchers who discovered and worked with radiation died from leukemia and other cancers. And so did many of the Japanese who survived the atomic bombs of World War II. Radiation is all around us. It can be defined as energy in invisible waves, and it comes from the sun and from outer space. It also comes from X rays and radioactive pollution. Most of it comes in very small doses.

Scientists once thought only large doses of radiation caused cancer. But they are finding out that people who build or test nuclear bombs or who live near nuclear testing sites or who work with radiation *in any way* seem to get cancer more often than other people. The trouble is, like chemicals, radiation takes a long time to cause cancer. It is hard to be sure a person has cancer because he or she worked with radiation twenty years before.

Melissa Cohen had several bad colds when she was just a baby. Her doctor thought treating her thymus gland with radiation from his X-ray machine might keep her from getting

While radiation is known to cause cancer, used carefully it can also help detect the disease. These chest X rays show a pair of healthy lungs (top) and those of a patient with lung cancer (bottom).

[19

more colds. The thymus gland is a small organ inside the chest, which helps a baby become immune to diseases. It shrinks as a person grows, but radiation shrinks it faster.

Somehow, researchers think, using radiation on the thymus damaged cells in the nearby thyroid gland in many babies and children. Years later, some of those damaged cells turned into cancers. Radiation probably caused Melissa's cancer. It may have caused Julie's, with or without help from a virus. It may even have helped to cause them all. No one knows.

THE BODY ITSELF

The fourth possible cause of cancer is the body itself. Researchers have found hints that some people may be pre-programmed, before they are born, to get cancer. They may have a special gene inside every cell that "tells" the body to start growing a cancer when it gets to be a certain age. This may be why a few kinds of cancer seem to run in families.

Another way the body helps cancer start is when its own immune system breaks down. Every normal person has an army of special cells to fight off infection and disease. Some researchers think these cells can also keep the body from getting cancer. This may be why most people never get it. But if the immune system stops working, the body loses its protection. Cancer gets a chance to start.

The only thing researchers are completely sure of is that there is no simple "cause" of cancer. Smoking causes cancer, but not in everyone who smokes. Radiation causes cancer, but only sometimes. Viruses can cause cancer, but not always. If cancer happened every time someone's immune system breaks down, everyone who gets sick would have cancer. And

[20

if everyone had a built-in cancer-causing gene, we would *all* die of cancer.

In fact, there are so many confusing "causes" of cancer, the most important question may not be why people get cancer, but why most people *don't*. Scientists are still looking for answers.

Chapter 5
THE CANCER SCOUTS

Cancer can be cured. Doctors know enough right now to cure at least half of all the new cases of cancer that occur. But only about one-third of the people who get cancer are actually cured. The rest die, mainly because their cancers are not discovered in time. To cure cancer, doctors must find it while it is still small, and before it spreads.

Unfortunately, there is no easy way to discover cancer in time. Cancer is called the "hidden killer" because it does not usually show any signs or symptoms until it has grown to a serious size.

The American Cancer Society is a large group of men and women who work to educate people about cancer, as well as to find ways to prevent, discover, and treat it. They publish a CAUTION list of seven danger signals everyone should watch for:

Change in bowel or bladder habits.
A sore that does not heal.
Unusual bleeding or discharge.

[22

Thickening or lump in breast or elsewhere.
Indigestion or difficulty in swallowing.
Obvious change in a wart or mole.
Nagging cough or hoarseness.

The trouble is, these are all signs which may—or may not—be symptoms of a large, growing cancer. Patients have a much better chance of being cured if their cancer is discovered *before* any of these symptoms happen.

Janice Hughes has none of the seven danger signals, but she just had her yearly physical checkup. As a part of the examination, her doctor did a Pap test, named after Dr. George Papanicolaou, who developed it.

Janice's doctor took loose cells from inside Janice's vagina, or birth canal, on a cotton swab and smeared them onto a glass slide. Laboratory technicians examined the cells under a microscope and discovered that a few were malignant. More tests showed that Janice had what doctors call a microinvasive carcinoma, which means a small, spreading cancer.

Another simple test which can discover early cancer is the proctoscope exam. With a specially designed viewer-and-flashlight tube called a proctoscope, a doctor can look inside a person's colon to check for signs of cancer. Cancer of the colon is the second most common cancer in middle-aged men and women.

An easy early test for the most common cancer in women is a breast self-examination. Every woman should examine her own breasts once a month, to watch for the tiny beginnings of a lump that could be cancer. But most early cancers are not easy to spot, and most patients are not so lucky as Janice. John Roberts' carcinoma was much more advanced when he first checked with his doctor. Because John smokes,

[23

his doctor suspected lung cancer right away. There were several tests he used to prove it.

First the doctor took a chest X ray and a sample of the sputum that came from John's lungs when he coughed. The X ray showed a dark shadow on the upper wall of John's left lung. It could mean cancer, or several other lung diseases. The sputum sample, checked under a microscope, did not show any cancer cells.

Next, the doctor used a bronchoscope to examine John's lung. A bronchoscope is a long flexible tube about the thickness of a pencil, with a light that shines from the tip. It slides in through the nose. Looking into the bronchoscope, the doctor could see all the way down John's throat and inside his lung. Blood-spotted mucus coated the walls. The doctor collected a sample and pulled it out through the tube. The doctor could also see John's lower lung. Parts of it looked twisted, as if something were pushing it out of shape.

Under the microscope, the mucus from John's lung showed small oat-shaped carcinoma cells—a dangerous kind of lung cancer. More X rays showed another cancer beginning in the other lung, and a suspicious shadow on the liver.

When Melissa Cohen began to feel a strange lump inside her neck, she went back to the doctor who had told her to "get more rest." This time, he sent her to a thyroid specialist.

The first thing the specialist, called an endocrinologist, did was take a complete medical history from Melissa. She asked questions about where Melissa had lived, about illnesses in her family, about exposure to radiation, and about her weight loss, her tiredness, whether or not she had trouble swallowing and whether or not her voice seemed hoarse.

The endocrinologist carefully examined Melissa's head and neck with her fingers, gently feeling the lump. She looked at Melissa's ears, nose, and throat, and she inspected her

[24

vocal cords with another lighted tube called a laryngoscope. Then she sent Melissa to the hospital for more tests. At the hospital, a surgeon carefully felt the lump. Then he used a needle to take a biopsy from Melissa's neck, which means he drew out some small bits of tissue, through the needle. The cells he drew out were malignant.

Afterward, a radiologist took X rays of Melissa's whole body. A tiny spot showed on Melissa's lung.

Kevin Howard's leg seemed to hurt more every day. His regular pediatrician examined the aching leg and sent him to a radiologist. A technician helping the radiologist took several X-ray pictures of the leg, from the front and from the sides. When the radiologist looked at them, he saw that the end of the thigh bone was twisted and misshapen. Thicker and thinner parts of the bone made a kind of sunburst picture on the X ray. To the radiologist, the picture looked exactly like cancer.

But an X ray is not enough proof. Kevin checked into the hospital, where a surgeon removed a small piece of the bone tumor. This is another way of doing a biopsy. It showed that Kevin had an osteogenic sarcoma, or bone cancer. Finally, the radiologist took a set of tomographic X rays of Kevin's whole body. The tiny cancer growing on his lung was too small to see.

Julie's nose was bleeding, again, and her doctor noticed the rash on her skin. Julie told him about the way her legs ached at night, and about how tired she felt all the time. The doctor took a small sample of blood from Julie's finger and examined it under a microscope. Her blood had too many white cells, and many of them looked strange and ragged. That could mean leukemia, but it could also mean an infection.

In the hospital, another doctor carefully drew out a sam-

[25

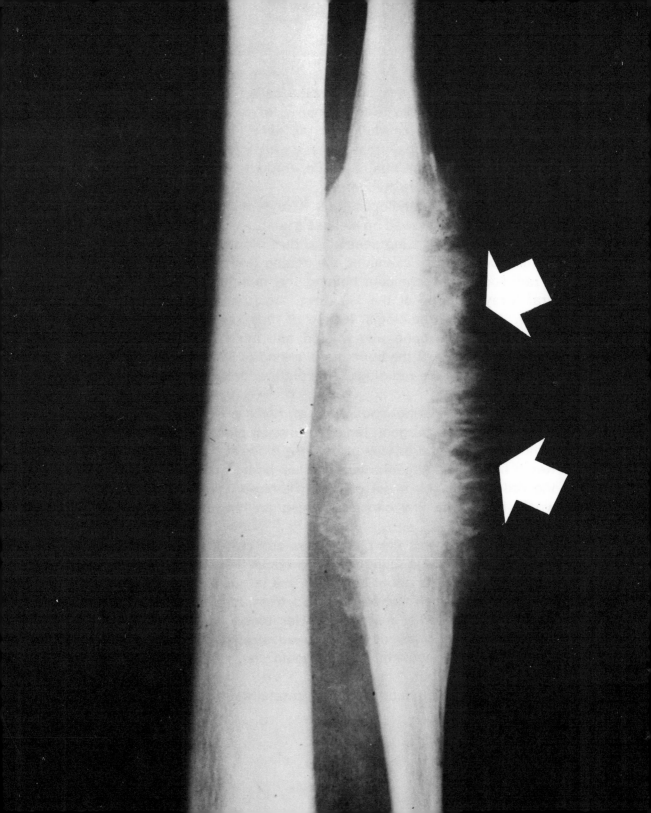

ple of the red bone marrow from Julie's breastbone. Under the microscope, the marrow cells showed that Julie had a cancer called acute lymphocytic leukemia, or "ALL."

Richard Waring's Hodgkin's disease was discovered by some of the same tests. He had X rays, blood tests, a bone marrow test, and several biopsies. The tests showed that Richard's cancer had spread to his spleen, liver, and stomach.

Every day, doctors use these tests and dozens of others to uncover new cases of cancer. But sometimes the best tests are not good enough. And sometimes, they can even be dangerous. For example, X rays can spot breast cancers too tiny for any woman or her doctor to feel, but X rays can also cause cancer. It is not safe to use them every year, on healthy persons. What doctors need is a safe, inexpensive, and trustworthy test that can discover all kinds of cancer from just a small sample of blood, and tell the doctors exactly where the cancer is located. Then everyone could be tested for cancer every year or so.

Such a test may be developed someday. Researchers are learning that some cancers produce special chemicals that get into the blood before the patient knows he or she is sick. Cancers of the colon, prostate, liver, and lungs often put chemicals into the blood. Researchers are looking for others.

Once a cancer has been discovered, doctors can begin to try and cure it. The next four chapters explain some of the methods they are using today.

An X ray showing osteogenic sarcoma, or bone cancer.

[27

Chapter 6
SURGERY AGAINST CANCER

Surgery is the oldest and still the most important treatment for cancer. Surgeons treat cancer by cutting it out of the body.

Surgery cures thousands of cancers every year. It works best on tumors which are small and local—all in one place. But even large cancers can sometimes be completely cut away, if they have not begun to spread. The cancers surgery cannot cure are the ones which have already started growing in other parts of the body, or which involve parts of the body a person can't do without.

Janice Hughes had an operation called a *radical hysterectomy.* To make sure he got every cancerous cell, the surgeon removed more than just the growth. He removed the whole cervix, uterus, and ovaries, the organs where babies grow and develop. Since every patient is different, other women with cancer of the cervix might have different treatment. Some might require more surgery, some might need less, and some might not have surgery at all.

The doctor thought he cut out all of Janice's cancer, but

he could not be sure. Since cancer often begins again in new places, he examined her several times after surgery. Finally, five years after the operation, the doctors pronounced Janice cured of cancer.

Melissa Cohen needed a different kind of surgery. Her cancer began in her thyroid, so her first operation was a thyroidectomy, to remove her whole thyroid gland. The surgeon also removed some lymph nodes and tissue from around the thyroid for testing. The tests showed that Melissa's cancer had spread outside her thyroid. A few days later, she had another operation to remove most of the lymph nodes and tissue from her neck. Then the surgeon sent Melissa back to her other doctors for more testing. He was still not sure that surgery had removed all of her cancer.

Kevin Howard's tumor was destroying the bone in his leg. Sometimes doctors can put in an artificial bone to replace what cancer has destroyed. This is what Kevin's doctor did, but his surgeon was still worried. He sent Kevin to another cancer specialist.

John's surgeon decided not to operate at all. Sometimes it is possible to cure lung cancer by cutting away part or even half of a patient's lungs. But John's doctors knew surgery would not cure him, because his cancer was spreading swiftly to all parts of his lungs and liver and probably to other places. Instead, they sent him to a radiologist.

Surgery could not help Richard or Julie. Richard's cancer had spread too far to be cured by removing a few lymph nodes, and Julie's cancer was in all of her bones and blood. There is no way to cut out a cancer that has spread all through the body.

Sometimes a new technique, or way of operating, helps surgeons do a better job. Many surgeons now use a

[29

microscope and special tiny instruments, to operate in parts of the body that are too small to see clearly with their eyes. Some cut with the light of a laser beam.

Other surgeons use a technique called cryosurgery. With an instrument much colder than ice, they freeze away tumors instead of cutting them. Cryosurgery sometimes has a special bonus for cancer patients. Normal surgery often seems to make small growths in other parts of the body grow faster. But cryosurgery may make them shrink or even fade away.

All surgeons agree that their biggest problem in curing cancer is getting the cancer cells that have slid away to new places. For those cancers, another kind of cure is needed.

Chapter 7
RADIATION AGAINST CANCER

Radiation can cause cancer, but it can also cure it. Radiation destroys cancer, cell by cell.

Like surgery, radiation is used to remove cancer from the body. But radiation can also destroy healthy cells. What radiologists try to do is find ways to injure and kill as many cancer cells as possible without hurting very many normal cells. This is not easy.

There are several different kinds of radiation. Some, like heat and light, are not normally dangerous, but they cannot cure cancer. The radiation that works against cancer is much more powerful.

Gamma rays come from radioactive atoms. They are like high-energy beams of light that cannot be seen. X rays are also high-energy beams of invisible radiation. In fact, they are almost exactly the same thing as gamma rays, but they come from the electrical energy inside a special machine.

X rays and gamma rays do several kinds of damage to cells. They seem to injure the DNA molecules inside the nu-

[31

cleus, which stops the cell from dividing. Because cancer cells divide more often than normal cells, they are harmed by radiation more often than normal cells.

A large dose of radiation can also kill healthy cells. It probably damages their outer membranes. But most cancer cells lie under healthy skin. Sometimes they are deep inside the body. The radiation has to pass through healthy cells on its way to the cancer.

One of the ways radiologists protect healthy cells is by spacing out the doses of radiation. A patient gets a radiation treatment once a day, for instance, and rests in between. Normal cells have time to heal themselves before the next treatment. Cancer cells are not able to heal themselves as quickly as normal cells do. More of them will die.

Another protection is to keep the patient, or the ray beam, moving. Radiologists can use a computer to aim a beam of X rays so carefully that they can hit a cancer the size of a pea from the front, back, and sides, one after the other, even though the cancer is deep inside the body. Moving beams protect the skin, because each section of skin gets only a small part of the whole radiation dose.

Since aiming the radiation beam right at the cancer is very important, a patient receiving radiation must lie perfectly still. Radiologists have developed a special way to help. They sometimes make a plaster cast of the whole body, or of the part of the body being treated. Then the patient can lie absolutely still inside this cast while the X ray works on his or her cancer.

Gamma rays do not come from a machine, so they can sometimes be placed right inside the cancer. Radioactive needles, made of radium, can treat growths from the inside out. Radioactive gold can be injected with a needle. And radioactive capsules can be placed inside body openings, to get closer to the growth. Other radioactive materials will hunt for certain kinds of tissue inside the body. Iodine always looks for thyroid cells, even when cancer has carried them to the lungs. Radioactive iodine is used to carry gamma rays to a thyroid cancer, without harming the skin.

Since surgery had not cured Melissa Cohen's thyroid cancer, her doctors tried radioactive iodine next. About a month after her operation, Melissa began radiation treatments. She drank a solution of iodine 131, which took gamma rays to the cancerous cells in her throat and in her lung. Iodine 131 can sometimes cure thyroid cancer, but Melissa's tumors kept growing. Her radiologist sent her to another kind of specialist.

John Roberts' lung cancer was too badly spread for surgery to treat successfully. The radiologist knew that he could not cure John, either, but he could make John more comfortable and help him to live a little longer.

X rays are very damaging to lung tissue. The radiologist carefully aimed his beam at the tumors in John's left lung, but he shielded the right lung. He had to leave part of the lung untreated, so that John could breathe.

After three weeks of radiation treatments, John began to feel better. His cough was not so painful, and he began to enjoy spending time with his family. In a few months, the cancer in John's left lung was almost completely destroyed, but so was John's left lung. And the cancer on his right lung was beginning to grow bigger. Without radiation, John would probably have already died. But radiation could not help him any longer. John's doctor sent him to another specialist.

Radiation often cures early cases of Hodgkin's disease, especially if the cancer stays in the lymph nodes of one small

[33

part of the body. Lymph nodes lie in a chain, and cancer spreads from one to the next to the next. To treat them, radiologists "outline" the chain of lymph nodes, using lead blocks shaped to fit around the rest of the body. Radiation cannot pass through lead, so the blocks protect the patient as the radiologist aims a beam of high-energy X rays at the skin over the malignant nodes.

But Richard's cancer had already spread all through his body. Radiation cannot help unless it has a specific target. Richard's radiologist sent him to a second specialist.

Kevin could have been treated with radiation for his osteosarcoma. Sometimes oncologists (cancer doctors) use radiation first, on a cancerous bone tumor. Then they wait a few months. If the growth shrinks completely away, they may not need to replace the bone. More often, they use radiation to make the tumor smaller before they operate. But Kevin's tumor was very fast-growing. His doctor thought immediate surgery was safer.

Unfortunately, the operation did not come soon enough. Four months later, Kevin had a growth on his lung. Radiologists treated Kevin's new lung cancer with X rays. It began to shrink, but the doctors were still worried. They sent Kevin to another specialist.

Sometimes it seems as if radiation treatments harm the patient more than they help. John and Kevin both had their skin burned badly. Julie lost most of her hair, and all three felt too sick to eat most of the time. But most doctors and patients believe that any treatment which helps fight cancer is worth the trouble, especially if it can save the patient's life.

Another kind of radiation treatment is now being tried, and it sometimes does a better job than X rays or gamma rays. This radiation is a stream of tiny particles called pions. Pions are much smaller than atoms. There are three kinds, but the ones used most often to treat cancer have a negative electrical charge. This tiny bit of electricity helps pions to stop inside a patient's body, while X rays and gamma rays go all the way through. It helps radiologists aim them so that they will deliver almost all of their energy right into the cancer cells.

But it takes huge, complicated machines called accelerators to produce pions, and they cost millions of dollars. Doctors are testing them on a few patients now, but it will be years before they are sure how well pions work. And if they work, it will be more years until there are enough accelerators to treat every patient who needs them.

Radiation can cure cancer. Many people are alive today because they had radiation treatments. But, like surgery, it can only work when the cancer is in one place. For other cancers, a different kind of cure is needed.

Chapter 8
DRUGS
AGAINST CANCER

Chemotherapy is the best treatment for cancers that surgery and radiation cannot cure. It means using drugs to fight cancer, and its name comes from the words "chemical" and "therapy," meaning "treatment."

Drugs have been curing other diseases for a long time. Most of them work by killing disease-causing bacteria. And since tiny bacteria are very different from human beings, it is not too hard to poison them without poisoning the patient. But cancer is not caused by a bacteria. Cancer is cells gone wild.

Cancers grow from normal human cells, and most drugs that can kill them kill healthy cells, too. Chemotherapists work with powerful poisonous drugs, and they use them very carefully.

Cells change as they become cancers. They do not look or act exactly the same as normal cells. Chemotherapists use these differences to plan ways for drugs to kill one more often than the other. For instance, cancer cells divide in two more often than ordinary cells do. And some cancer cells need spe-

[36

cial "foods," or nutrients, that other cells can make for themselves. Different kinds of drugs work to keep them from dividing or from getting the nutrients they need.

Alkylating agents are one kind of cancer-fighting drug. These strong chemicals are often called "cell poisons." They were discovered when doctors noticed that poisonous mustard gas seemed to stop cells from dividing inside its victims. Alkylating agents start a chemical reaction inside cells. Sometimes they cause DNA chains to break apart and rejoin in strange ways. When this happens, the cell cannot divide. The problem is, alkylating agents do not work just on cancer cells. They can destroy all kinds of cells that divide often. Cells in the bone marrow, the blood, the hair and other places can be hurt. Too much can poison the whole body. Doctors use these drugs against leukemia, breast cancer, Hodgkin's disease, and other cancers.

Antimetabolites are drugs that stop cells from getting the nutrients they need. Researchers say an antimetabolite is like a key that fits into a lock but will not turn. It fills up the "lock" in a cancer cell so that the right "key," or nutrient, cannot get inside. In other words, an antimetabolite kills a cell by taking the place of something it needs.

Some *antibiotics* work against cancers. These are related to the bacteria-killing antibiotics such as penicillin, but they are stronger and more poisonous. Cancer-killing antibiotics seem to attach themselves to DNA and RNA molecules inside cells and keep the cells from making copies of them. Without new DNA and RNA, cells cannot divide.

With surgery and radiation, the most important question is not how big a cancer is, but how far it has spread. Chemotherapy is the opposite. It can seek out and kill cancer cells in almost all parts of the body, but it is not good at attacking

[37

large growths, or clumps of cells. This is why chemotherapy is often used together with surgery or radiation. After the big growth has been removed, chemotherapy can find and destroy the stray cancer cells that are left behind.

Unfortunately, it is not often that easy. Drugs cannot hurt some cancer cells at all. Other cancer cells begin to build up an immunity to the poisonous drugs. That means that after a while the drugs stop working. This is one reason so many drugs are needed. When one drug stops working, the doctor can try another kind. Sometimes several drugs are used at once. The idea is to kill as many cancer cells as possible, as quickly as possible, without killing the patient.

Julie Farrow's leukemia is one of the most serious kinds of cancer. Not long ago, everyone who got leukemia died. Some children died only a few months after they discovered that they were sick.

Julie went to a big cancer hospital in the city, where an oncologist started her on three strong drugs right away. These drugs fight cancer in three different ways, but they made Julie feel sicker than ever.

Prednisone pills are *hormones,* which are natural body chemicals. Prednisone stops cancerous white cells from

Top: leukemic blood cells. Note the irregular shape of the cells and the large size of the nucleus as compared to the total cell size. Bottom: leukemic blood cells partially rejuvenated by chemotherapy.

[38

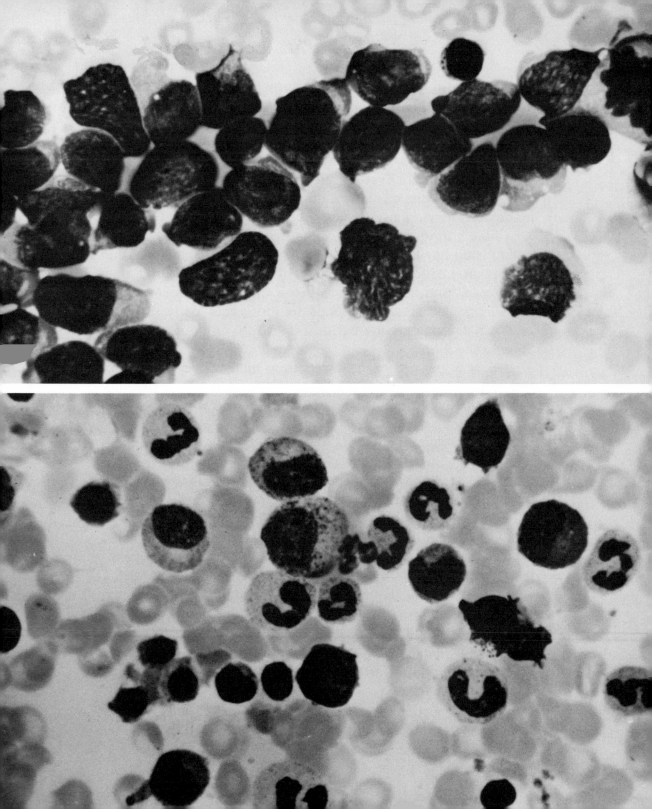

growing, but it also made Julie's body look puffy and fat. She took the pills every day.

Every week, Julie had injections of a drug called vincristine, made from the periwinkle flower. Vincristine can stop cancer cells from dividing, but it stung and it made her fingers and toes feel numb. Every three weeks, the doctor injected her with an antibiotic called daunorubicin. It also stung, and it made Julie nauseous.

Julie's long hair began to fall out as the drugs injured cells inside her body. Loss of hair, numbness, puffiness, and nausea are called side effects. There are others, and they happen as long as the person takes the drugs because cancer-killing drugs are poisonous to the whole body. But unpleasant side effects are better than dying. Without the drugs, Julie would die.

After a few weeks, chemotherapy had destroyed most of the cancer cells in Julie's blood and bone marrow. But leukemia cells can hide in the brain, and the brain has a built-in barrier to keep drugs out.

To kill cancer cells in Julie's brain, her oncologist did two things. She injected a drug called methotrexate into Julie's spine, because the spine carries drugs directly into the brain. She also sent Julie to a radiologist, who used radiation to kill the last remaining cancer cells. (See Chapter 7.)

Finally, Julie was in remission. To leukemia specialists, "remission" means that all signs of leukemia have disappeared from the body. Julie look methotrexate pills every week to keep her cancer from coming back. She took them for two years. Julie has been in remission for five years, now, and she is feeling fine.

Julie is not taking any medication now, so all the side effects caused by the drugs have gone away. Her hair has grown back, and she looks slim and healthy. She swims and plays tennis with her friends, and this year she is a starter on the school's girl basketball team.

Not all leukemia patients are so lucky. Many of them never go into remission. Somehow, their cancers are stronger than the drugs. And in some other patients, leukemia comes back. But some leukemia patients have been in remission for more than ten years. Doctors hope that they are permanently cured, and Julie's doctor believes that she is one of them.

Kevin Howard was not so lucky. After his surgery had healed, the doctors tried huge doses of methotrexate, hoping to kill whatever cancer cells were left in his body. They also gave him a "rescue drug" as an antidote. Methotrexate is so poisonous that large doses can kill the patient quicker than his cancer can. But the doctors suspected that the methotrexate was not working. They sent Kevin to another specialist.

Chemotherapy helped John Roberts. He began taking a drug called cyclophosphamide and two of the drugs Julie took —vincristine and prednisone. The drugs caused the cancer in his right lung to shrink. John felt well for most of the next year. Every three weeks, he went to the hospital for more cancer-killing drugs. Finally, his cancer began to grow again. John's doctor sent him to a doctor who specialized in a new and experimental kind of cancer treatment.

Richard went on a chemotherapy plan called MOPP (M, O, P, and P are the initials of the drugs used in the plan.) The MOPP plan has helped more than half of the patients with Hodgkin's disease to live longer. Many of them have lived for five years or more, and some may be permanently cured of cancer. But Richard's cancer was too strong for the drugs. About a year later, Richard Waring died.

Chemotherapy could not help Melissa for very long. An

antibiotic called bleomycin made the new cancers in her neck shrink, but they grew back. Soon after that, Melissa died.

Chemotherapy is a fairly new treatment for cancer, and doctors are learning more about it all the time. A few years ago, chemotherapy was only used for patients who were already dying. Now, it can sometimes cure cancer completely, and it can help in thousands of cases that it cannot cure. New drugs and new ways to use the drugs they already have are making chemotherapists more important in the fight against cancer.

But some cancers cannot be cured by surgery, radiation, or drugs. The body needs another kind of defense against such cancers.

Chapter 9
THE BODY'S OWN DEFENDER CELLS

The body has an army of defender cells to protect itself from illness. These special cells destroy germs and invading viruses. They can even fight cancer—sometimes. This may be the reason most people never get cancer. These defender cells belong to the *immune system,* which is one of the most complicated parts of the body. No one completely understands how the immune system works.

"Immune" means "protected from harm." The system includes a large number of special cells and chemicals which the body makes and uses to attack enemies. Every minute of the day, the immune system protects the body from invading germs and diseases. Most of the time, it does a good job. But the body's immune system does not always work, and scientists are trying to find out why. They hope that learning more about how the body prevents and cures disease will give them a new weapon to use against cancer.

Macrophages are the scavenger cells. Their name means "big eater," because they can wrap themselves around enemy

[43

cells or particles and "eat" them. They clean up after the defender cells, getting rid of dead cells and tissue.

Lymphocytes are white blood cells, and they come in several varieties. B and T cells are the most important. They both begin as something called a stem cell, inside bone marrow. Then they "grow up" to do different jobs.

B cells react to *antigens.* An antigen is the name for anything which starts a B cell working. When B cells discover a strange bacteria inside the body, they react to the unfamiliar antigens on it. They begin to make new proteins called *antibodies,* that are especially designed to fight each different antigen. Antibodies lock themselves onto antigens and hold them prisoner.

Viruses also have antigens, and B cells make special antibodies to fight each one. Then they store a few, for future use. The reason a person can have chicken pox only once, for instance, is that the second time a chicken pox virus tries to invade the body, stored antibodies are ready to pounce on it.

T cells begin just like B cells, but they travel to the chest and pass through the thymus. The thymus (see Chapter 4) is a tiny gland that shrinks as a person grows. Its main job seems to be turning immune cells into fighters.

The T cells can attack and kill bacteria or any other cells they recognize as foreign to the body. They patrol through the blood and tissues, looking for enemies. T cells can work alone, or they can team up with B cells or macrophages, or even with each other. Many scientists think they often recognize and kill new cancer cells before they have a chance to start a growth.

But if that is true, then why do cancers start? How do they escape the patrolling T cells? Right now, no one knows for

[44

sure. Researchers all over the world are trying to find out, and they have several ideas.

One idea is that something must go wrong with the immune system before a cancer can start. There is some proof for this. People who have to take drugs that block out their immune system get cancer more often than other people. (Doctors use drugs to slow down the immune system when they transplant kidneys or hearts from one person to another. Otherwise, the immune system would destroy the new organ.)

Also, older people, whose immune system no longer works as well as it did, get cancer much more often than younger people. Their T cells may be too weak to handle cancer.

However, even though doctors do not understand exactly how the immune system works, they are already using it to help cancer patients live longer. Their ideas and methods keep changing as they learn more.

Chemotherapy put Julie into remission. Her leukemia went away. To help keep her cancer from coming back, an immunologist made scratches on Julie's skin and rubbed on a substance called BCG.

BCG stands for "bacillus Calmette-Geurin," the name for a very weak bacteria something like the one which causes tuberculosis in cows. Somehow, in people, BCG seems to perk up the whole immune system. Doctors hope it will help Julie's immune system find and destroy any new cancer cells that appear.

BCG has helped many patients with Hodgkin's disease. Richard was given BCG along with his chemotherapy. But sometimes chemotherapy and immunotherapy seem to work against each other. The drugs work against the immune system, while the BCG tries to build it up.

[45

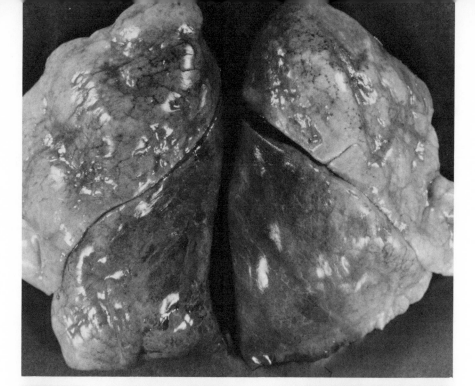
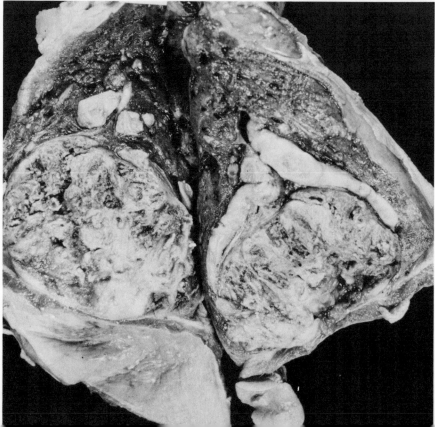

Richard's cancer was too far along for either treatment to cure. After a few months, Richard died.

John Roberts became part of a group experiment. The doctors knew that every person in the group was dying of lung cancer, but they wanted to find out if immunotherapy could help them to live longer. Researchers divided the group in half. One half, called the control group, got normal chemotherapy. The other half, including John, were given normal chemotherapy plus a new kind of treatment.

Every medical experiment must have a control group. They are treated exactly the same as the experimental group, except that they do not get the new treatment being tested. Then doctors can compare the two groups to see if the new medication worked better.

Besides chemotherapy, John's group were given weekly injections of a bacteria called C. parvum. The C. parvum were dead, so they were not able to start any new illnesses. But their bodies seemed to "wake up" the immune systems inside John and the other patients.

After three months, almost a third of the control group had died. All of John's group were still alive. Six months later, most of the control patients were dead, but almost all of the experimental group were alive. Some of their lung and liver tumors had stopped growing. A few had even begun to

Human lungs. Non-cancerous
(top) and cancerous (bottom).
The two large, light, circular
areas at the bottom of the
cancerous lungs are tumors.

shrink. Unfortunately, the improvement did not last. Most of the cancers soon began growing again.

After another six months, John died. But a few members of his group were still alive, long after all the "controls" had died. The experiment showed that patients with oat cell carcinoma could live twice as long with immunotherapy as without it.

Now, almost all lung cancer patients get some kind of immunotherapy. A few may even have been cured. Before immunotherapy, they probably would have died. BCG and C. parvum cause immune cells to react. The body carries that reaction over to fight the cancer.

Another kind of immunotherapy transfers one person's immunity into another. For example, Kevin Howard's doctor took blood samples from his parents and his brother and sister. The doctor found that Kevin's brother had a natural immunity against Kevin's cancer cells.

The doctor took lymphocytes from the brother's blood and used them to make a treatment called transfer factor. Transfer factor is an unusual kind of protein the body makes to protect itself from illness. Injecting it into Kevin might possibly help keep his cancer from returning. But Kevin's cancer had already returned, inside his lung.

Transfer factor has saved the lives of some patients with osteogenic sarcomas, but it cannot be used when cancer has already spread to the lungs. A few months later, Kevin died. Kevin's doctor might have tried immunotherapy earlier. Some doctors use BCG with chemotherapy and radiation as soon as they discover a bone cancer. Then, with the cancer under control, they can use surgery to take out just the malignant part of the bone. They can replace it with a substitute and save the patient's arm or leg.

[48

BCG could also have helped with Kevin's lung cancer, if the new cancer had been discovered in time. If they get the best treatment, quickly enough, more than half of the patients with Kevin's kind of cancer can now be saved.

These are only a few of the different kinds of immunotherapy being tried or studied today. Another hope is a chemical called interferon, a protein the white blood cells make to fight against viruses. It seems to stimulate the immune system and attack even tumor cells. Scientists hope that it will soon play an important part in fighting cancer.

Immunotherapy is the newest and least understood way of treating cancer. Right now, it does not do as good a job as surgery, radiation, or chemotherapy. Sometimes, in fact, immunotherapy seems to make cancers grow faster. A few patients have died from experiments with immunotherapy.

But immunotherapy works in a different way from the other cancer treatments. It tries to work *with* the body to destroy cancer instead of cutting or burning or poisoning it away. Many doctors think immunotherapy may someday be the best treatment of all.

And even more important, immunotherapy may someday find a way to prevent cancer, the way vaccinations prevent polio and measles. But first, scientists must learn exactly how the immune system works. That is why the most important field of cancer control is research.

[49

Chapter 10
RESEARCH: FIGHTING FOR THE FUTURE

If doctors knew all about what cancer is and how it works, they could probably cure it almost all of the time. In fact, they could probably prevent most of the cancers that happen today.

But researchers in all parts of the world are working to learn all they can about cancer. Every year, new bits and pieces of information are discovered in hospitals and laboratories and inside mice and dogs and tiny cells.

Cancer research is a complex and confusing field. It has workers who are physicians, molecular biologists, virologists, nuclear biophysicists, biochemists, and even computer technologists. Here are just a few of the ways they study cancer.

First, scientists can grow cancer cells in a dish. In fact, if they are handled carefully, cancer cells divide and grow in laboratory dishes even better than they do in people. They can live for years. Working with individual cells helps researchers study the way they look and act. Technicians can cut cells into thin slices and examine them under the electron microscope to see how they look inside. They can take pictures of cells dividing and even of cells turning into cancers.

Scientists often test new treatments on cancer cells to see what kills or injures them. New ideas take years of testing before they are ready to be tried on humans. Some turn into useful treatments, and some never work.

The next step in most cancer research is animal testing. Scientists use all kinds of animals, but mice are the most popular. They are small, and they live their lives much faster than larger animals. Since cancer happens most often in old age, researchers need an animal that gets old quickly. Usually, they breed special mice for their experiments. Some strains, or families, of mice almost always get certain kinds of cancer. Other strains are bred so that they all have almost the same genes, like identical twins. Cells can be passed from one of these mice to another without altering the immune system.

Researchers use animals to test foods and chemicals to see if they cause cancer. You may have heard stories about rats which got cancer after drinking can after can of soda pop per day. Researchers do give large doses of whatever they are testing to the animals, but for a good reason. Testing with large doses acts as a magnifying glass. If small amounts of something give cancer to one or two mice in a thousand, it might be hard to spot. But if huge doses of that same something cause cancer in five hundred mice, everyone notices.

Scientists want to prevent as many cancers in people as possible. If large amounts of a food can cause many rat cancers, it is possible that even small amounts will give cancer to some people. But do the same things that cause cancer in mice also cause cancer in humans? Some do and some don't. Usually, researchers try the experiment again, on larger animals, to be sure.

Animal testing has also helped to discover another, even more confusing cause of cancer: stress. For years, doctors had noticed that many of their cancer patients seemed nervous and upset most of the time, even before they knew they had cancer. Researchers wondered if stress might cause cancer or help it to grow. They began to test the idea on mice.

They took two groups of mice which almost always developed breast cancer and put them in separate rooms. The control group was treated the usual way. They lived in noisy metal cages with wire floors. They were handled often and given injections and blood tests. As researchers expected, ninety out of one hundred developed breast cancer.

The other mice were put in cozy plastic cages with wood shavings on the floor. The room was kept dark and quiet, and the mice were handled very gently. The results were astonishing. Only seven out of one hundred mice got cancer. No one is quite sure what these results mean in relation to people. Scientists still have a lot to learn about the way stress affects cancer. But all laboratory animals are treated more carefully now. Careful handling matters.

But pet animals get cancer, too. Some research units look for pet dogs who have cancer. Doctors try experimental cures on them, working as carefully as they would on a human. Sometimes the pet is cured or helped, and the doctors can use what they learn to help people.

Finally, all new treatments for cancer have to be tried on human patients. Testing is almost always done with two groups, the way immunotherapy was tried on John Roberts and other lung cancer patients.

Unfortunately, the better cancer treatments get, the harder it is to test new ones. With animals, scientists can give no treatment at all to the control group. But all human patients must get the best kind of treatment there is, even if it confuses the test results. Usually that means several different kinds of chemotherapy, plus immunotherapy, surgery, and radiation. With all those treatments going on, it is hard for doctors to tell what medication is doing what.

Preventing cancer is better than curing it. The last important field of research is looking for some kind of vaccine to protect people from cancer. There has been some progress. Right now, it is possible to vaccinate cats against leukemia and mice against some other specific cancers. But the "specific" part is the problem. Since cancer is more than one hundred different diseases, it would be almost impossible to protect everyone against all of them. A few human patients, after surgery, have been vaccinated against their own lung cancer. Doctors hope the vaccine will keep cancer from coming back. It seems to be working, but it is too soon to be sure.

Every year, millions of dollars are spent on cancer research. Sometimes large amounts of money are spent on ideas that don't work. But every discovery helps, even if it only proves that an old (or new) idea about cancer is wrong. There is still a long way to go, but most researchers think someday cancer will be conquered. Maybe it will be in your lifetime.

Chapter 11
CANCER AND YOU

In 1900, heart disease, pneumonia, tuberculosis, and influenza were the biggest killers in the United States. In 1979, most Americans who died, died from heart disease or cancer. In 1950, no one heard much about cancer. Now we hear about it all the time. Movie stars and other famous people who have cancer are in the news often.

What is the difference? Are more people getting cancer now than before? Yes and no. Like everything else about cancer, there is no simple answer. Yes, more people are getting cancer, but no, most cancer is not really increasing. For one thing, there are more people now, and we are healthier and live longer than people did in 1900. The big killers of that year are not as dangerous now as they were then. And since older people are more apt to get cancer, there are more cancers now than there used to be.

But for every hundred thousand Americans, the number who will die from cancer has not changed very much in the last fifty years, except for two kinds. The good news is stomach cancer. Once it was a serious killer. Now it is almost rare. Researchers think changes in what people eat is preventing it. The bad news is lung cancer. Once it was rare, but in 1980, more than one hundred thousand people will get it. Most of them will die. Lung cancer alone is the main reason there are more cases of cancer every year. Researchers are convinced that most of it is due to smoking.

But the most important reason we hear more about cancer today is because people want to talk about it. They want to know what is happening and what they can do to protect themselves. A few people are afraid to try. "Just about everything causes cancer," they say, "so what's the use? We may as well give up." But scientists know that isn't true. There are several simple things everyone can do to guard against the most common kinds of cancer, and to help their chances of being cured if they do get it.

This book is too short to explain all the reasons behind these ideas for prevention, but most researchers would agree with them. They are not guarantees, but they are certainly worth a try. First, and most important, don't smoke. Smoking causes more cancers than any other single thing. It causes cancers in the lungs, the bladder, the pancreas, the lip, the esophagus, and several other places.

Second, eat a well-balanced diet. That doesn't mean becoming a vegetarian or giving up all "junk food" forever. It just means being careful to get some of all the foods your body needs, without too much of any one thing. Eating too much fat, for instance, may cause colon and breast cancers— the two most common kinds next to cancer of the lung.

Third, be careful with chemicals. No one knows yet how many chemicals can cause cancer, but people are learning to be more careful of all of them. Where you work or play, watch out for strange smells or pollution that gets on your skin.

[55

Two thousand cigarettes, piled on the table,
will produce the amount of tobacco tar shown in the flask.

Bladder cancers, lymphomas, or other cancers might be the result.

Here are a few more things to look out for:

X rays—don't have any you don't really need.

The sun—tan gently and don't broil yourself. Too much sun, especially in young people, can cause cancers ten or twenty years later.

Uncleanliness—poor hygiene can cause cancer. Remember the chimney sweeps and cancer of the scrotum.

But if cancer attacks anyway, there are still ways that you can help fight it. First, get to a doctor quickly. Most cancer patients know something is wrong with their body for months before they see a doctor. Many of them die because they waited. Second, choose the right doctor. No doctor is an expert about everything, and cancer is the most confusing disease of all.

Of the six patients described in this book, Julie got the best care. She went to a special cancer center, where oncologists knew about the latest treatments. Melissa and Kevin might have lived if they had seen a cancer specialist sooner.

Cancer care is changing so fast that by the time you read this, there will probably be better ways to treat many kinds of cancer. But not all doctors will know them. Not every patient can go to a special cancer hospital or research unit. There isn't room. But oncologists in those units work with thousands of other doctors in all parts of the country, trying to make sure they have the latest information. Every doctor who treats cancer should be in touch with them.

"Cancerphobia" is the fear of cancer. Sometimes it can be almost as deadly as cancer itself. It makes people afraid to get help, and it makes them give up. Being afraid can't prevent or cure cancer, but being careful can. Cancer can be conquered, *if everyone helps.*

[57

Glossary

ALKYLATING AGENT—A chemical that destroys cancer cells by reacting with their DNA.

ANTIBIOTIC—A bacteria-killing drug that works against cancer cells by stopping their DNA from reproducing itself.

ANTIBODY—A protein that the body forms to protect itself from antigens. It is sometimes called an "immune body."

ANTIGEN—An unusual or foreign substance inside the body that causes an antibody to form.

ANTIMETABOLITE—A drug that resembles a nutrient which cancer cells need. It kills cancer cells by interfering with their growth.

CARCINOGEN—A substance that causes cancer.

CARCINOMA—A form of cancer that begins in the covering or lining of the organs of the body, including the skin. It is the most common form of cancer.

CELL MEMBRANE—A thin layer of protein that protects the outside of animal cells, letting necessary chemicals pass in and out.

CHEMOTHERAPY—Treatment of disease using drugs and other chemicals.

CHROMOSOMES—Thread-like structures inside a cell's nucleus that carry genes.

CYTOPLASM—A gray or colorless jelly made of protein that forms the living part of a cell outside the nucleus.

DEOXYRIBONUCLEIC ACID (DNA)—A complex, spiral-shaped molecule that contains all the information a cell needs to reproduce itself.

GENE—The basic unit of inheritance that passes on characteristics of living organisms from one generation to the next.

HORMONES—Chemicals that help regulate the body's functions. They can help destroy some cancer cells by suppressing cell growth.

IMMUNE SYSTEM—The body substances that fight disease and infection.

LEUKEMIA—A form of cancer that begins in the blood-making tissues of the body.

LEUKOCYTES—White blood cells. There are many different kinds.

LYMPHOCYTE—The most important kind of cell in the body's lymph system. It fights infection.

LYMPHOMA—A form of cancer that begins in the body's lymph nodes.

MACROPHAGE—A large blood cell that helps keep the body clean by destroying dead or foreign cells.

NUCLEOTIDES—The compounds that make up DNA. In these compounds are chemicals arranged in a code, to carry information.

NUCLEUS—The specialized part of each cell that holds the chromosomes and regulates the cell's activities.

ONCOLOGY—The study of cancer.

ORGANELLES—Tiny sacs inside a cell's cytoplasm, organelles do specialized jobs such as manufacturing or storing chemicals.

SARCOMA—A form of cancer that begins in bone, fat, muscle, or connective tissue.

TUMOR—A swelling or an abnormal growth of tissue.

For Further Reading

Heintze, Carl. *A Million Locks and Keys; The Story of Immunology.* New York: Hawthorne Books, 1969

Kelly, Patricia. *The Mighty Human Cell.* New York: The John Day Co., 1967

Silverstein, Alvin and Virginia. *Cancer.* Revised Edition. New York: The John Day Co., 1977

Sonnett, Sherry. *Smoking.* New York: Franklin Watts, 1977

U.S. Department of Health, Education and Welfare, *The Cancer Story.* Publication #78–232, 1978

Index

Alkylating agents, 37
American Cancer Society, 22
Antibiotics, 37
Antibodies, 44
Antigens, 44
Antimetabolites, 37

Bacillus Calmette-Geruin (BCG), 45,
    48–49
Benign, 7
Biopsy, 25
Blood, 9–10
    composition of, 9
    leukocyte, 9–10
    platelet, 9
    samples, 11
Body as a cause of cancer, 20–21
    immune system, 20
    inherited characteristics, 20
Brain, treatment of, 40
Breast cancer, 16

Breast self-examination, 23
Bronchoscope, 24

Cancer
    care, 57
    causes, 14, 52
    characteristics, 12
    combined therapy, 38
    cure rate, 22
    current awareness, 55
    danger signals, 22–23
    definition of, 2
    increase in, 54
    kinds, 9
    mortality rate, 13
    prevention, 53, 55–57
    research, 47, 50–53
    testing, 23–27
    treatment, 28–30, 31–35, 36–41,
        45–49
Cancer cells, 5–6, 36

Cancerphobia, 57
Carcinogen, 15
Carcinomas, 8, 9, 23
Cells, 3–6
    cell membrane, 3–4
    division of, 5
Cervix, 9
Chemicals as a cause of cancer, 15–16
    smoking, 15
    work-related causes, 15–16
Chemotherapy, 36–41
    Hodgkin's disease, 41
    leukemia, 38–41
    lung cancer, 41
    side effects, 38–40
Chromosomes, 4
Colon cancer, 16
Cytoplasm, 4

Danger signals, 22–23
Deoxyribonucleic acid (DNA), 5, 17, 37
Diethylstilbestrol (DES), 16

Genes, 4–5

Hodgkin's disease, 12
    chemotherapy, 41
    radiation treatment, 33–34
    testing for, 27
Hooke, Robert, 3

Immune system, 20, 43–45
Immunity to drugs, 38
Immunotherapy, 45–49
    interferon, 49
    research, 47
    transfer factor, 48–49

Leukemia, 9, 16–17
    acute lymphocytic leukemia (ALL), 27
    blood cells, 39
    remission, 40
    signs of, 25
    treatment, 38–41
Lung cancer, 16
    chemotherapy, 41
    increase in, 55
    oat-cell carcinoma, 24, 47–48
    radiation treatment, 33
Lymphocytes, 44
Lymphomas, 9

Macrophages, 43–44
Malignant, 7
Mesothelioma, 16

Nucleus of a cell, 4
Nutrition, 55

Oncologist, 7, 34
Organelles, 4
Osteogenic sarcoma, 12, 26

Pap test, 23
Pions, 34–35
Pott, Sir Percival, 14
Precancerous cells, 15
Proctoscope exam, 23

Radiation as a cause of cancer, 19–20

Radiation treatment, 31–35
    accelerators, 35
    dosage, 32
    Hodgkin's disease, 33–34
    iodine, 33
    lung cancer, 33
    radium needles, 32–33
    side effects, 34
Remission, 40
Research, 47, 50–53
    animal testing, 51–53
    control group, 47
    funds, 53
RNA, 17, 37

Sarcomas, 9
Smoking, 15, 16, 55–56
Stomach cancer, 54–55
Stress as a cause of cancer, 52
Sun exposure, 57
Surgery, 28–30
    cryosurgery, 30
    disadvantages, 29

microscopic, 30
radical hysterectomy, 28
thyroidectomy, 29

Testing, 23–27
    biopsy, 25
    bone marrow test, 27
    breast self-examination, 23
    bronchoscope, 24
    Pap test, 23
    proctoscope exam, 23
    sputum sample, 24
    x rays, 24–25
Thymus gland, 20, 44
Thyroid gland, 8
Tumor, 7

Virogene, 17
Viruses as a cause of cancer, 16–17

X rays, 24–25, 27
    chest, 18, 24
    tomographic, 25

616.9   Haines, Gail Kay
Hai   Cancer

616.99   Haines, Gail Kay
Hai   Cancer